CONTENTS

VEGETARIAN DELIGHTS 61

DESSERTS 85

SOUPS AND STARTERS

Jota (Bean and Sauerkraut Soup)

Servings: 4

Time: 1.5 hours

Ingredients:

- 1 cup dried white beans, soaked overnight
- 1 onion, finely chopped
- 2 cloves garlic, minced
- 1 cup sauerkraut, drained and rinsed
- 2 potatoes, peeled and diced
- 1 medium carrot, sliced
- 1 smoked pork sausage, sliced

- 2 tablespoons tomato paste
- 1 bay leaf
- Salt and pepper to taste
- 1 tablespoon oil
- Fresh parsley for garnish

Directions:

1. In a large pot, heat oil over medium heat. Sauté onions and garlic until golden.
2. Add sliced sausage, sauté until browned.
3. Stir in tomato paste, sauerkraut, potatoes, carrots, and soaked beans. Mix well.
4. Pour in enough water to cover the ingredients. Add bay leaf, salt, and pepper.
5. Bring to a boil, then reduce heat and simmer for 1 hour or until beans are tender.
6. Adjust seasoning if needed. Serve hot, garnished with fresh parsley.

Matevž (Potato and Bean Stew)

Servings: 6

Time: 1.5 hours

Ingredients:

- 1 cup dried pinto beans, soaked overnight
- 4 large potatoes, peeled and diced
- 1 onion, finely chopped
- 2 cloves garlic, minced
- 2 tablespoons vegetable oil
- 1 smoked ham hock
- Salt and pepper to taste
- Fresh parsley for garnish

Directions:

1. In a large pot, heat oil over medium heat. Sauté onions and garlic until translucent.
2. Add soaked beans, potatoes, and smoked ham hock. Cover with water and bring to a boil.
3. Reduce heat, cover, and simmer for about 1 hour or until beans and potatoes are tender.
4. Remove ham hock, shred the meat, and return it to the pot. Season with salt and pepper.

5. **Serve hot, garnished with fresh parsley.**

Žganci with Mushroom Sauce (Buckwheat Mush with Mushroom Sauce)

Servings: 4

Time: 45 minutes

Ingredients: *For Žganci (Buckwheat Mush):*

- **2 cups buckwheat flour**
- **1 teaspoon salt**
- **Water**

For Mushroom Sauce:

- **2 cups mixed mushrooms, sliced**
- **1 onion, finely chopped**
- **2 cloves garlic, minced**
- **2 tablespoons butter**
- **1 cup vegetable broth**
- **Salt and pepper to taste**
- **Fresh chives for garnish**

Directions: *For Žganci:*

1. **Mix buckwheat flour with salt in a bowl. Gradually add water, stirring until a thick batter forms.**

2. Drop spoonfuls of batter into boiling salted water. Cook until Žganci rise to the surface.
3. Drain and keep warm.

For Mushroom Sauce: **4. In a pan, sauté onions and garlic in butter until softened.**

5. Add mushrooms and cook until browned.
6. Pour in vegetable broth, simmer for 10 minutes. Season with salt and pepper.
7. Serve Žganci topped with mushroom sauce and garnished with fresh chives.

Prežganka (Thickened Broth with Crackers)

Servings: 4

Time: 30 minutes

Ingredients:

- 4 cups chicken or vegetable broth
- 3 tablespoons all-purpose flour
- 2 tablespoons butter
- 4 round crackers
- Salt and pepper to taste
- Chopped fresh chives for garnish

Directions:

1. In a saucepan, heat the broth until it simmers.
2. In a separate pan, melt butter over medium heat. Add flour and stir continuously to make a roux.
3. Cook the roux for 2-3 minutes until it turns golden but not browned.
4. Gradually whisk in the hot broth, ensuring no lumps form. Continue to whisk until the mixture thickens.
5. Season with salt and pepper to taste.
6. Crush the round crackers into the thickened broth and stir until well combined.

7. Simmer for an additional 5 minutes, allowing the crackers to absorb some of the broth.

8. Serve hot, garnished with chopped fresh chives.

Bujta Repa (Turnip and Pork Stew)

Servings: 6

Time: 2 hours

Ingredients:

- 1 kg turnips, peeled and diced
- 500g pork shoulder, cubed
- 1 large onion, finely chopped
- 2 cloves garlic, minced
- 2 tablespoons lard or vegetable oil
- 1 teaspoon caraway seeds
- 2 bay leaves
- Salt and pepper to taste
- Fresh parsley for garnish

Directions:

1. In a large pot, heat lard or vegetable oil over medium heat. Sauté onions and garlic until softened.
2. Add cubed pork shoulder and brown on all sides.
3. Stir in caraway seeds and diced turnips. Mix well.
4. Pour in enough water to cover the ingredients. Add bay leaves, salt, and pepper.

5. Bring to a boil, then reduce heat and simmer for 1.5 to 2 hours or until pork and turnips are tender.

6. Adjust seasoning if needed. Serve hot, garnished with fresh parsley.

Šelinka (Barley and Vegetable Soup)

Servings: 4

Time: 1 hour

Ingredients:

- 1 cup pearl barley, rinsed
- 1 onion, finely chopped
- 2 carrots, diced
- 2 potatoes, peeled and cubed
- 1 leek, sliced
- 1 celery stalk, chopped
- 1 bay leaf
- 4 cups vegetable broth
- Salt and pepper to taste
- Fresh dill for garnish

Directions:

1. In a large pot, combine pearl barley and vegetable broth. Bring to a boil and simmer for 30 minutes.
2. In a separate pan, sauté onions until translucent.
3. Add carrots, potatoes, leek, and celery to the sautéed onions. Cook for an additional 5 minutes.

4. Transfer the sautéed vegetables to the pot with barley and broth.

5. Add a bay leaf, salt, and pepper. Simmer for another 20-30 minutes until barley and vegetables are tender.

6. Adjust seasoning if needed. Remove the bay leaf.

7. Serve hot, garnished with fresh dill.

Kisla Juha (Sour Turnip Soup)

Servings: 4

Time: 1.5 hours

Ingredients:

- 1 kg turnips, peeled and grated
- 1 onion, finely chopped
- 2 cloves garlic, minced
- 2 potatoes, peeled and diced
- 1 carrot, sliced
- 1 parsnip, sliced
- 1 celery root, diced
- 1 bay leaf
- 1 tablespoon vegetable oil
- 1 tablespoon vinegar
- Salt and pepper to taste
- Fresh parsley for garnish

Directions:

1. In a large pot, heat vegetable oil over medium heat. Sauté onions and garlic until translucent.
2. Add grated turnips, potatoes, carrot, parsnip, and celery root. Stir well.

3. Pour in enough water to cover the vegetables. Add a bay leaf, vinegar, salt, and pepper.

4. Bring to a boil, then reduce heat and simmer for 1 to 1.5 hours until the vegetables are tender.

5. Adjust seasoning if needed. Remove the bay leaf.

6. Serve hot, garnished with fresh parsley.

Krompirjeva Juha (Potato Soup)

Servings: 6

Time: 45 minutes

Ingredients:

- 4 large potatoes, peeled and diced
- 1 onion, finely chopped
- 2 cloves garlic, minced
- 1 carrot, sliced
- 1 leek, sliced
- 1 celery stalk, chopped
- 6 cups vegetable or chicken broth
- 2 tablespoons butter
- 1/2 cup heavy cream
- Salt and pepper to taste
- Fresh chives for garnish

Directions:

1. In a large pot, melt butter over medium heat. Sauté onions and garlic until translucent.
2. Add diced potatoes, carrot, leek, and celery. Stir well.

3. Pour in the vegetable or chicken broth. Bring to a boil, then reduce heat and simmer for 25-30 minutes or until potatoes are tender.

4. Use an immersion blender to partially blend the soup, leaving some chunks for texture.

5. Stir in heavy cream and season with salt and pepper. Simmer for an additional 5 minutes.

6. Adjust seasoning if needed. Serve hot, garnished with fresh chives.

Ajmoht (Barley and Bean Soup)

Servings: 6

Time: 1.5 hours

Ingredients:

- 1 cup pearl barley, rinsed
- 1 cup dried beans (your choice), soaked overnight
- 1 onion, finely chopped
- 2 carrots, diced
- 2 celery stalks, chopped
- 2 cloves garlic, minced
- 1 bay leaf
- 2 tablespoons vegetable oil
- 6 cups vegetable or beef broth
- Salt and pepper to taste
- Fresh parsley for garnish

Directions:

1. In a large pot, heat vegetable oil over medium heat. Sauté onions and garlic until translucent.
2. Add diced carrots, celery, and drained soaked beans. Stir well.

3. Pour in vegetable or beef broth. Add rinsed pearl barley and a bay leaf.

4. Bring to a boil, then reduce heat and simmer for 1 to 1.5 hours until barley and beans are tender.

5. Season with salt and pepper to taste. Remove the bay leaf.

6. Serve hot, garnished with fresh parsley.

Kašna (Barley and Vegetable Stew)

Servings: 4

Time: 1.5 hours

Ingredients:

- 1 cup pearl barley, rinsed
- 1 onion, finely chopped
- 2 carrots, diced
- 2 potatoes, peeled and diced
- 1 parsnip, sliced
- 1 leek, sliced
- 2 cloves garlic, minced
- 2 tablespoons vegetable oil
- 1 bay leaf
- 4 cups vegetable broth
- Salt and pepper to taste
- Fresh thyme for garnish

Directions:

1. In a large pot, heat vegetable oil over medium heat. Sauté onions and garlic until translucent.
2. Add diced carrots, potatoes, parsnip, and leek. Stir well.

3. Pour in vegetable broth. Add rinsed pearl barley and a bay leaf.

4. Bring to a boil, then reduce heat and simmer for 1 to 1.5 hours until barley and vegetables are tender.

5. Season with salt and pepper to taste. Remove the bay leaf.

6. Serve hot, garnished with fresh thyme.

MAIN COURSES - MEAT

Kranjska Klobasa (Carniolan Sausage)

Servings: 4

Time: 2 hours (including resting time)

Ingredients:

- 500g pork shoulder, finely ground
- 250g bacon, finely chopped
- 1 cup ice water
- 2 cloves garlic, minced
- 1 teaspoon black pepper, freshly ground
- 1 teaspoon caraway seeds
- 1 teaspoon salt

- Natural hog casings (soaked and cleaned)

Directions:

1. In a large mixing bowl, combine ground pork, chopped bacon, minced garlic, black pepper, caraway seeds, and salt.
2. Gradually add ice water to the mixture, stirring until well combined. Ensure the mixture has a sticky texture.
3. Rinse the hog casings thoroughly and soak them in warm water.
4. Stuff the sausage mixture into the casings, tying them off at 6-inch intervals.
5. Twist the sausages into 6-inch links.
6. Bring a large pot of water to a simmer (not boiling). Add the sausages and poach for about 20-30 minutes.
7. Allow the sausages to cool. Once cooled, refrigerate for at least an hour.
8. Grill or pan-fry the sausages until golden brown and cooked through.
9. Serve hot with mustard and fresh bread.

Idrijski Žlikrofi (Idrija-style Dumplings) with Meat Filling

Servings: 4

Time: 2 hours (including resting time)

Ingredients: *For the Dough:*

- 2 cups all-purpose flour
- 2 eggs
- 1/2 teaspoon salt
- Water, as needed

For the Meat Filling:

- 300g ground pork
- 1 onion, finely chopped
- 2 cloves garlic, minced
- 2 tablespoons vegetable oil
- 1 teaspoon marjoram
- Salt and pepper to taste

Directions: *For the Dough:*

1. In a large bowl, combine flour, eggs, and salt.
2. Gradually add water and knead until a smooth, elastic dough forms. Cover and let it rest for 30 minutes.

23

For the Meat Filling: **3. In a pan, heat vegetable oil over medium heat. Sauté onions and garlic until translucent.**

4. Add ground pork and cook until browned. Season with marjoram, salt, and pepper. Allow it to cool.

Assembling the Dumplings: **5. Roll out the dough thinly on a floured surface.**

6. Cut out rounds using a glass or a round cutter.
7. Place a small amount of the meat filling in the center of each round.
8. Fold the dough over the filling, creating a crescent shape, and seal the edges.
9. Bring a large pot of salted water to a boil. Cook the dumplings until they float to the surface (about 5-7 minutes).
10. Remove with a slotted spoon and serve hot.

Pražen Krompir s Slanino (Roasted Potatoes with Bacon)

Servings: 4

Time: 45 minutes

Ingredients:

- 4 large potatoes, peeled and diced
- 200g bacon, diced
- 1 onion, finely chopped
- 2 tablespoons vegetable oil
- Salt and pepper to taste
- Chopped fresh parsley for garnish

Directions:

1. Preheat the oven to 200°C (392°F).
2. In a large oven-safe pan, heat vegetable oil over medium heat.
3. Add diced potatoes and cook until golden brown and slightly crispy.
4. Push the potatoes to the side and add diced bacon and chopped onions to the pan. Cook until bacon is crispy and onions are translucent.

5. Mix the bacon and onions with the roasted potatoes, ensuring even distribution.

6. Season with salt and pepper to taste. Transfer the pan to the preheated oven.

7. Roast for an additional 15-20 minutes or until the potatoes are fully cooked and crispy.

8. Remove from the oven, garnish with chopped fresh parsley, and serve hot.

Kosilo iz Pečenega Piščanca (Roast Chicken Lunch)

Servings: 4

Time: 2 hours

Ingredients:

- 1 whole chicken (about 1.5 kg)
- 4 tablespoons olive oil
- 2 teaspoons paprika
- 1 teaspoon dried rosemary
- 1 teaspoon dried thyme
- Salt and pepper to taste
- 4 large potatoes, peeled and quartered
- 4 carrots, peeled and sliced
- 1 onion, cut into wedges
- 4 cloves garlic, whole
- Fresh parsley for garnish

Directions:

1. Preheat the oven to 180°C (356°F).
2. Rinse the chicken inside and out, pat dry with paper towels.

3. Rub the chicken with olive oil, paprika, dried rosemary, dried thyme, salt, and pepper, ensuring an even coating.

4. In a roasting pan, arrange the chicken in the center and surround it with quartered potatoes, sliced carrots, onion wedges, and whole garlic cloves.

5. Roast in the preheated oven for about 1.5 to 2 hours or until the chicken reaches an internal temperature of 75°C (167°F) and the vegetables are golden and tender.

6. Baste the chicken with its juices halfway through the cooking time.

7. Once done, let the chicken rest for 10 minutes before carving.

8. Garnish with fresh parsley and serve hot with roasted vegetables.

Ocvrti Sir (Fried Cheese)

Servings: 4

Time: 30 minutes

Ingredients:

- 200g semi-hard cheese (like Gouda or Emmental), sliced into 1/2-inch thick rectangles
- 1 cup all-purpose flour
- 2 eggs, beaten
- 1 cup breadcrumbs
- Vegetable oil for frying
- Salt and pepper to taste
- Lemon wedges for serving

Directions:

1. Set up a breading station with three shallow bowls: one with flour, one with beaten eggs, and one with breadcrumbs.
2. Dip each cheese slice into the flour, shaking off excess.
3. Next, dip the floured cheese into the beaten eggs, ensuring it's well-coated.
4. Finally, coat the cheese with breadcrumbs, pressing them onto the surface for an even coating.

5. Heat vegetable oil in a pan over medium-high heat.

6. Fry the breaded cheese slices for about 2-3 minutes on each side or until golden brown and crispy.

7. Remove from the pan and place on a paper towel to absorb excess oil.

8. Season with salt and pepper to taste.

9. Serve hot with lemon wedges on the side.

Pohorski Lonec (Pohorje Pot) - Meat and Vegetable Stew

Servings: 6

Time: 2 hours

Ingredients:

- 500g beef stew meat, cubed
- 200g smoked pork ribs
- 2 tablespoons vegetable oil
- 1 onion, finely chopped
- 2 cloves garlic, minced
- 2 carrots, sliced
- 2 potatoes, peeled and diced
- 1 parsnip, sliced
- 1 leek, sliced
- 1 celery root, diced
- 2 bay leaves
- 1 teaspoon marjoram
- Salt and pepper to taste
- 1 liter beef broth
- 1/2 cup red wine (optional)
- Fresh parsley for garnish

Directions:

1. In a large pot, heat vegetable oil over medium heat. Sear beef stew meat and smoked pork ribs until browned on all sides.
2. Add chopped onions and garlic, sauté until onions are translucent.
3. Pour in the beef broth and red wine (if using). Bring to a simmer.
4. Add carrots, potatoes, parsnip, leek, celery root, bay leaves, marjoram, salt, and pepper.
5. Cover the pot and simmer on low heat for about 1.5 to 2 hours or until the meat is tender.
6. Adjust seasoning if needed. Remove the bay leaves.
7. Serve hot, garnished with fresh parsley.

Svinjska Pečenka z Zelišči (Roast Pork with Herbs)

Servings: 6

Time: 2.5 hours

Ingredients:

- 1.5 kg pork loin or shoulder, bone-in
- 3 cloves garlic, minced
- 2 tablespoons olive oil
- 1 tablespoon Dijon mustard
- 1 tablespoon fresh rosemary, chopped
- 1 tablespoon fresh thyme, chopped
- 1 tablespoon fresh sage, chopped
- Salt and pepper to taste
- 1 cup chicken or vegetable broth
- 1/2 cup white wine (optional)
- 2 tablespoons all-purpose flour (for gravy)

Directions:

1. Preheat the oven to 180°C (356°F).
2. In a small bowl, mix minced garlic, olive oil, Dijon mustard, chopped rosemary, thyme, and sage to create a herb paste.

3. Make deep incisions into the pork and rub the herb paste all over, ensuring it gets into the incisions. Season generously with salt and pepper.

4. Place the pork in a roasting pan and add chicken or vegetable broth and white wine (if using) to the pan.

5. Roast in the preheated oven for about 2 to 2.5 hours, basting the pork with pan juices every 30 minutes.

6. Once the internal temperature reaches 70°C (158°F) and the skin is crispy, remove from the oven and let it rest for 15 minutes before carving.

7. While the pork rests, prepare gravy: In a small saucepan, mix 2 tablespoons of flour with a bit of water to create a smooth paste. Whisk into the pan juices and cook until thickened.

8. Carve the roast pork, serve hot with the herb-infused gravy.

Ješprenj (Buckwheat with Smoked Meat)

Servings: 4

Time: 1.5 hours

Ingredients:

- 2 cups buckwheat groats
- 200g smoked pork ribs or bacon, diced
- 1 onion, finely chopped
- 2 cloves garlic, minced
- 1 carrot, grated
- 1 celery stalk, chopped
- 1 bay leaf
- 4 cups beef or vegetable broth
- Salt and pepper to taste
- Fresh parsley for garnish

Directions:

1. Rinse the buckwheat groats under cold water and drain.
2. In a large pot, sauté diced smoked pork ribs or bacon until browned and crispy.
3. Add chopped onions and garlic, sauté until onions are translucent.

4. Stir in grated carrot and chopped celery, cook for an additional 2-3 minutes.

5. Add rinsed buckwheat groats to the pot. Stir well to combine with the other ingredients.

6. Pour in beef or vegetable broth, add a bay leaf, salt, and pepper.

7. Bring to a boil, then reduce heat to low, cover, and simmer for about 30-40 minutes or until buckwheat is tender.

8. Remove the bay leaf. Adjust seasoning if needed.

9. Serve hot, garnished with fresh parsley.

Krvavica (Blood Sausage) with Sauerkraut

Servings: 4

Time: 1.5 hours

Ingredients:

- 4 blood sausages (Krvavica)
- 500g sauerkraut, drained
- 1 onion, finely chopped
- 2 tablespoons vegetable oil
- 1 apple, peeled and grated
- 1 teaspoon caraway seeds
- Salt and pepper to taste
- Fresh parsley for garnish

Directions:

1. In a large pan, heat vegetable oil over medium heat. Add chopped onions and sauté until translucent.
2. Add sauerkraut to the pan, along with grated apple and caraway seeds. Stir well.
3. Cook the sauerkraut mixture for about 20-30 minutes until it's tender and the flavors meld together.
4. While the sauerkraut cooks, preheat the oven to 180°C (356°F).

5. Prick the blood sausages with a fork to prevent bursting while cooking. Place them on a baking sheet.

6. Bake the blood sausages in the preheated oven for about 30 minutes or until fully cooked.

7. Serve the blood sausages hot alongside the sauerkraut mixture.

8. Garnish with fresh parsley and season with salt and pepper to taste.

Svinjska Rolada (Pork Roulade) with Mustard Sauce

Servings: 4

Time: 2 hours

Ingredients:

For the Pork Roulade:

- 600g pork loin, butterflied
- 150g bacon, thinly sliced
- 1 onion, finely chopped
- 2 cloves garlic, minced
- 2 tablespoons Dijon mustard
- 2 tablespoons fresh parsley, chopped
- Salt and pepper to taste
- Kitchen twine

For the Mustard Sauce:

- 1 cup chicken broth
- 2 tablespoons Dijon mustard
- 1 tablespoon flour
- 2 tablespoons butter
- Salt and pepper to taste

Directions:

Preparing the Pork Roulade:

1. Preheat the oven to 180°C (356°F).
2. Lay the butterflied pork loin on a flat surface. Season with salt and pepper.
3. Spread Dijon mustard over the pork, leaving a border around the edges.
4. Sprinkle chopped onions, minced garlic, and fresh parsley over the mustard.
5. Lay the bacon slices evenly over the mustard-covered pork.
6. Roll the pork loin tightly, starting from one end. Secure with kitchen twine at intervals.
7. Season the outside of the roulade with salt and pepper.
8. In a large pan, sear the pork roulade on all sides until browned.
9. Transfer the seared roulade to a baking dish and roast in the preheated oven for about 1.5 hours or until fully cooked.

Preparing the Mustard Sauce: 10. In a saucepan, melt butter over medium heat. Add flour and whisk until smooth.

11. Gradually whisk in chicken broth and Dijon mustard.

12. Continue whisking until the sauce thickens. Season with salt and pepper to taste.

Serving: 13. Slice the pork roulade into rounds and serve with mustard sauce.

MAIN COURSES - FISH

Postrv na Žaru (Grilled Trout)

Servings: 2

Time: 30 minutes

Ingredients:

- 2 whole trout, cleaned and scaled
- 2 tablespoons olive oil
- 1 lemon, thinly sliced
- 4 sprigs fresh rosemary
- Salt and pepper to taste
- Fresh parsley for garnish

Directions:

1. Preheat the grill to medium-high heat.

2. Rinse the trout under cold water and pat dry with paper towels.

3. Make three diagonal slashes on each side of the trout to help it cook evenly.

4. Rub the outside and cavity of each trout with olive oil. Season generously with salt and pepper.

5. Stuff the cavity of each trout with lemon slices and fresh rosemary sprigs.

6. Place the trout on the preheated grill and cook for about 5-7 minutes per side or until the flesh is opaque and flakes easily.

7. Carefully remove the trout from the grill and transfer to a serving platter.

8. Garnish with fresh parsley and serve hot.

Štruklji s Skušo (Strudel with Mackerel)

Servings: 4

Time: 1.5 hours

Ingredients:

For the Dough:

- 2 cups all-purpose flour
- 1 cup lukewarm water
- 2 tablespoons vegetable oil
- Pinch of salt

For the Filling:

- 4 fresh mackerel fillets, deboned and flaked
- 1 onion, finely chopped
- 2 tablespoons olive oil
- 1/2 cup breadcrumbs
- 1/4 cup fresh parsley, chopped
- Salt and pepper to taste

Directions:

Preparing the Dough:

1. In a large mixing bowl, combine flour, lukewarm water, vegetable oil, and a pinch of salt.

2. Knead the dough until it becomes smooth and elastic. Let it rest for 30 minutes.

Preparing the Filling: 3. In a pan, heat olive oil over medium heat. Add chopped onions and sauté until translucent.

4. Add flaked mackerel to the pan and cook until the fish is cooked through.

5. Stir in breadcrumbs and fresh parsley. Season with salt and pepper. Set aside to cool.

Assembling the Strudel: 6. Preheat the oven to 180°C (356°F).

7. Roll out the rested dough into a thin rectangle on a floured surface.

8. Spread the mackerel filling evenly over the rolled-out dough.

9. Roll the dough into a log, sealing the edges.

10. Place the strudel on a baking sheet and bake in the preheated oven for about 30-40 minutes or until golden brown.

11. Remove from the oven and let it cool for a few minutes before slicing.

Sardele v Beli Omaki (Sardines in White Sauce)

Servings: 4

Time: 30 minutes

Ingredients:

- 8 fresh sardines, cleaned and gutted
- 2 tablespoons olive oil
- 1 onion, finely chopped
- 2 cloves garlic, minced
- 2 tablespoons all-purpose flour
- 1 cup milk
- 1/2 cup dry white wine
- 1 lemon, juiced
- Salt and pepper to taste
- Fresh parsley for garnish

Directions:

1. Preheat the oven to 180°C (356°F).
2. In a pan, heat olive oil over medium heat. Add chopped onions and sauté until translucent.
3. Add minced garlic to the pan and cook for an additional minute.

4. Sprinkle flour over the onions and garlic, stirring continuously to create a roux.

5. Gradually add milk, stirring constantly to avoid lumps.

6. Pour in the white wine and lemon juice. Continue stirring until the sauce thickens.

7. Season the sauce with salt and pepper to taste. Set aside.

8. Place the cleaned sardines in a baking dish.

9. Pour the white sauce over the sardines, ensuring they are well-coated.

10. Bake in the preheated oven for about 15-20 minutes or until the sardines are cooked through.

11. Garnish with fresh parsley before serving.

Ribičev Brodet (Fisherman's Stew)

Servings: 4

Time: 1.5 hours

Ingredients:

- 500g mixed white fish fillets (such as sea bass, cod, and hake), cut into chunks
- 300g shrimp, peeled and deveined
- 2 tablespoons olive oil
- 1 onion, finely chopped
- 2 cloves garlic, minced
- 1 bell pepper, sliced
- 1 large tomato, diced
- 200ml dry white wine
- 400ml fish or vegetable broth
- 1 bay leaf
- 1 teaspoon dried thyme
- Salt and pepper to taste
- Fresh parsley for garnish
- Crusty bread for serving

Directions:

1. In a large pot, heat olive oil over medium heat. Add chopped onions and sauté until translucent.

2. Add minced garlic to the pot and cook for an additional minute.

3. Stir in sliced bell pepper and diced tomato. Cook until the vegetables are softened.

4. Pour in the dry white wine and allow it to simmer for a few minutes to reduce.

5. Add fish or vegetable broth to the pot. Bring to a gentle simmer.

6. Carefully place the fish chunks and shrimp into the simmering broth.

7. Add a bay leaf and dried thyme. Season with salt and pepper to taste.

8. Simmer the stew for about 15-20 minutes or until the fish is cooked through and the shrimp are pink.

9. Remove the bay leaf and discard.

10. Serve the Fisherman's Stew hot, garnished with fresh parsley, and accompanied by crusty bread.

Oslič na Žaru (Grilled Hake)

Servings: 4

Time: 30 minutes

Ingredients:

- 4 hake fillets
- 3 tablespoons olive oil
- 2 cloves garlic, minced
- 1 lemon, juiced
- 1 teaspoon dried oregano
- Salt and pepper to taste
- Fresh parsley for garnish
- Lemon wedges for serving

Directions:

1. Preheat the grill to medium-high heat.
2. In a small bowl, mix olive oil, minced garlic, lemon juice, dried oregano, salt, and pepper to create a marinade.
3. Pat the hake fillets dry with paper towels and place them in a shallow dish.
4. Pour the marinade over the hake fillets, ensuring they are well-coated. Allow them to marinate for at least 15 minutes.

5. Place the marinated hake fillets on the preheated grill. Grill for about 4-5 minutes per side or until the fish is opaque and easily flakes with a fork.

6. Transfer the grilled hake fillets to a serving platter.

7. Garnish with fresh parsley and serve hot with lemon wedges on the side.

Razne Ribje Jedi (Various Fish Dishes)

Servings: 4

Time: 45 minutes

Ingredients:

For the Fish Marinade:

- 1 lb mixed fish fillets (such as trout, perch, or catfish)
- Juice of 1 lemon
- 2 tablespoons olive oil
- 2 cloves garlic, minced
- 1 teaspoon dried oregano
- Salt and pepper to taste

For Grilled Fish:

- 1 lemon, sliced
- Fresh parsley, chopped for garnish

For Baked Fish Parcels:

- 4 sheets of parchment paper
- Mixed vegetables (bell peppers, zucchini, cherry tomatoes)
- Fresh dill, chopped for garnish

For Pan-Seared Fish:

- 2 tablespoons butter
- Lemon wedges for serving

Directions:

Fish Marinade:

1. In a bowl, mix lemon juice, olive oil, minced garlic, dried oregano, salt, and pepper.
2. Place the mixed fish fillets in the marinade, ensuring they are well coated. Let them marinate for at least 15 minutes.

Grilled Fish: 3. Preheat the grill. Grill the marinated fish fillets for 3-4 minutes per side or until fully cooked.

4. Garnish with lemon slices and chopped fresh parsley.

Baked Fish Parcels: 5. Preheat the oven to 375°F (190°C).

6. Place each marinated fish fillet on a parchment paper sheet. Top with mixed vegetables.
7. Fold the parchment paper to create sealed parcels.
8. Bake in the preheated oven for 15-20 minutes.
9. Garnish with chopped fresh dill.

Pan-Seared Fish: 10. In a skillet, melt butter over medium-high heat. Pan-sear the marinated fish fillets for 3-4 minutes per side or until golden brown.

11. Serve with lemon wedges on the side.

Rakci na Žaru (Grilled Crayfish)

Servings: 4

Time: 30 minutes

Ingredients:

- 12 crayfish, cleaned and halved
- 1/4 cup olive oil
- 2 cloves garlic, minced
- 1 lemon, juiced
- 1 teaspoon paprika
- 1 teaspoon dried thyme
- Salt and pepper to taste
- Fresh parsley for garnish
- Lemon wedges for serving

Directions:

1. Preheat the grill to medium-high heat.
2. In a small bowl, mix olive oil, minced garlic, lemon juice, paprika, dried thyme, salt, and pepper to create a marinade.
3. Place the halved crayfish in a large bowl and drizzle the marinade over them. Toss to coat evenly and let them marinate for about 15-20 minutes.

4. Skewer the crayfish onto metal or soaked wooden skewers, ensuring they are secure.

5. Place the skewers on the preheated grill and cook for about 3-4 minutes per side or until the crayfish shells turn bright red and the meat is opaque.

6. Transfer the grilled crayfish to a serving platter.

7. Garnish with fresh parsley and serve hot with lemon wedges on the side.

Morski List s Tartufi (Sea Bass with Truffles)

Servings: 4

Time: 45 minutes

Ingredients:

- 4 sea bass fillets
- 2 tablespoons olive oil
- 2 cloves garlic, minced
- 2 tablespoons fresh truffles, finely chopped
- 1/4 cup white wine
- 1/2 cup fish or vegetable broth
- Salt and pepper to taste
- Fresh parsley for garnish
- Truffle oil (optional)

Directions:

1. Preheat the oven to 180°C (356°F).
2. In a large oven-safe pan, heat olive oil over medium heat.
3. Season the sea bass fillets with salt and pepper.
4. Sear the sea bass fillets in the pan, skin side down, for 2-3 minutes or until the skin is crispy.

5. Flip the fillets and add minced garlic to the pan. Cook for an additional 2 minutes.

6. Sprinkle the chopped fresh truffles over the sea bass fillets.

7. Pour in white wine and fish or vegetable broth. Bring to a simmer.

8. Transfer the pan to the preheated oven and bake for about 15-20 minutes or until the sea bass is cooked through.

9. Remove from the oven and garnish with fresh parsley.

10. Optionally, drizzle truffle oil over the sea bass before serving.

11. Serve hot, with any remaining sauce spooned over the top.

Lignji na Žaru (Grilled Squid)

Servings: 4

Time: 30 minutes

Ingredients:

- 4 whole squid, cleaned
- 1/4 cup olive oil
- 2 cloves garlic, minced
- Zest and juice of 1 lemon
- 1 teaspoon dried oregano
- Salt and pepper to taste
- Fresh parsley for garnish
- Lemon wedges for serving

Directions:

1. Preheat the grill to medium-high heat.
2. In a small bowl, mix olive oil, minced garlic, lemon zest, lemon juice, dried oregano, salt, and pepper to create a marinade.
3. Pat the cleaned squid dry with paper towels.
4. Score the squid bodies in a crisscross pattern, being careful not to cut all the way through.

5. Place the squid in a shallow dish and brush the marinade over them, making sure to get the marinade into the scored areas.

6. Grill the squid for about 2-3 minutes per side or until they are opaque and have grill marks.

7. Transfer the grilled squid to a serving platter.

8. Garnish with fresh parsley and serve hot with lemon wedges on the side.

Krompir s Sardele (Potatoes with Anchovies)

Servings: 4

Time: 45 minutes

Ingredients:

- 4 large potatoes, peeled and diced
- 2 tablespoons olive oil
- 1 onion, finely chopped
- 2 cloves garlic, minced
- 8-10 anchovy fillets, chopped
- 1 teaspoon dried rosemary
- Salt and pepper to taste
- Fresh parsley for garnish

Directions:

1. Place the diced potatoes in a pot of salted water and boil until just tender. Drain and set aside.
2. In a large pan, heat olive oil over medium heat.
3. Add chopped onions to the pan and sauté until translucent.
4. Add minced garlic to the pan and cook for an additional minute.

5. Stir in the chopped anchovy fillets and cook until they dissolve into the mixture.

6. Add the boiled potatoes to the pan, tossing to coat them evenly with the anchovy mixture.

7. Sprinkle dried rosemary over the potatoes and continue cooking for 5-7 minutes until the potatoes are golden and crispy.

8. Season with salt and pepper to taste. Toss to combine.

9. Garnish with fresh parsley before serving.

VEGETARIAN DELIGHTS

Štruklji s Skuto (Cottage Cheese Strudel)

Servings: 6

Time: 1.5 hours

Ingredients:

For the Dough:

- **2 cups all-purpose flour**
- **1 cup lukewarm milk**
- **2 tablespoons vegetable oil**
- **Pinch of salt**

For the Filling:

- 2 cups cottage cheese (skuta)
- 1/2 cup sugar
- 1 egg
- 1 teaspoon vanilla extract
- Zest of 1 lemon

For the Topping:

- 2 tablespoons butter, melted
- 2 tablespoons breadcrumbs
- Powdered sugar for dusting

Directions:

Preparing the Dough:

1. In a large mixing bowl, combine flour, lukewarm milk, vegetable oil, and a pinch of salt.
2. Knead the dough until it becomes smooth and elastic. Let it rest for 30 minutes.

Preparing the Filling: **3. In a separate bowl, mix cottage cheese, sugar, egg, vanilla extract, and lemon zest until well combined.**

Assembling the Štruklji: **4. Preheat the oven to 180°C (356°F).**

5. On a floured surface, roll out the rested dough into a thin rectangle.

6. Spread the cottage cheese filling evenly over the rolled-out dough.

7. Roll the dough into a log, sealing the edges.

8. Place the strudel on a baking sheet lined with parchment paper.

Adding the Topping: 9. Brush the melted butter over the strudel.

10. Sprinkle breadcrumbs on top of the buttered strudel.

Baking and Serving: 11. Bake in the preheated oven for about 25-30 minutes or until the strudel is golden brown.

12. Remove from the oven and let it cool for a few minutes before slicing.

13. Dust with powdered sugar before serving.

Bela Pita z Zelenjavo (White Pizza with Vegetables)

Servings: 4

Time: 45 minutes

Ingredients:

For the Pizza Dough:

- 2 1/4 teaspoons (1 packet) active dry yeast
- 1 cup warm water
- 3 cups all-purpose flour
- 2 tablespoons olive oil
- 1 teaspoon sugar
- 1 teaspoon salt

For the Topping:

- 1 cup ricotta cheese
- 1 cup mozzarella cheese, shredded
- 1 zucchini, thinly sliced
- 1 bell pepper, thinly sliced
- 1 small red onion, thinly sliced
- 1 cup cherry tomatoes, halved
- 2 cloves garlic, minced

- 2 tablespoons olive oil
- Fresh basil leaves for garnish
- Salt and pepper to taste

Directions:

Preparing the Pizza Dough:

1. In a small bowl, combine warm water, sugar, and active dry yeast. Let it sit for 5-10 minutes until it becomes frothy.
2. In a large mixing bowl, combine flour and salt. Make a well in the center.
3. Pour the yeast mixture and olive oil into the well. Mix until a dough forms.
4. Knead the dough on a floured surface for about 5-7 minutes, then place it in a greased bowl. Cover and let it rise in a warm place for 1 hour or until doubled in size.

Assembling and Baking: **5. Preheat the oven to 220°C (425°F).**

6. Roll out the pizza dough on a floured surface to your desired thickness.
7. Transfer the rolled-out dough to a pizza stone or baking sheet.

8. In a bowl, mix ricotta cheese, minced garlic, salt, and pepper. Spread this mixture over the pizza dough.

9. Sprinkle shredded mozzarella over the ricotta layer.

10. Arrange zucchini, bell pepper, red onion, and cherry tomatoes on top.

11. Drizzle olive oil over the vegetables.

12. Bake in the preheated oven for 15-20 minutes or until the crust is golden and the cheese is bubbly.

13. Remove from the oven and let it cool for a few minutes.

14. Garnish with fresh basil leaves.

Pražena Zelenjava z Bučnim Omasom (Sautéed Vegetables with Pumpkin Sauce)

Servings: 4

Time: 30 minutes

Ingredients:

For the Pumpkin Sauce:

- 1 cup pumpkin puree
- 1/2 cup vegetable broth
- 2 tablespoons olive oil
- 2 cloves garlic, minced
- 1 teaspoon dried thyme
- Salt and pepper to taste

For the Sautéed Vegetables:

- 2 cups mixed vegetables (e.g., bell peppers, zucchini, cherry tomatoes), sliced
- 1 onion, thinly sliced
- 2 tablespoons olive oil
- Salt and pepper to taste
- Fresh parsley for garnish

Directions:

Preparing the Pumpkin Sauce:

1. In a saucepan, heat olive oil over medium heat.
2. Add minced garlic and sauté until fragrant.
3. Stir in pumpkin puree and vegetable broth.
4. Season with dried thyme, salt, and pepper.
5. Simmer the sauce for 5-7 minutes, allowing the flavors to meld. Set aside.

Sautéing the Vegetables: **6. In a large pan, heat olive oil over medium-high heat.**

7. Add sliced onions to the pan and sauté until translucent.
8. Add the mixed vegetables to the pan and sauté until they are tender yet still vibrant.
9. Season with salt and pepper to taste.

Combining and Serving: **10. Pour the pumpkin sauce over the sautéed vegetables in the pan.**

11. Toss gently to coat the vegetables in the pumpkin sauce.
12. Allow the mixture to simmer for an additional 2-3 minutes.
13. Garnish with fresh parsley before serving.

Špinačni Kaneloni (Spinach Cannelloni)

Servings: 4

Time: 1.5 hours (including baking time)

Ingredients:

- 12 cannelloni tubes
- 2 cups fresh spinach, chopped
- 1 cup ricotta cheese
- 1 cup shredded mozzarella cheese
- 1/2 cup grated Parmesan cheese
- 1 egg, beaten
- 2 cloves garlic, minced
- 1 teaspoon dried oregano
- Salt and pepper to taste

For the Tomato Sauce:

- 2 cups tomato passata or crushed tomatoes
- 1 tablespoon olive oil
- 1 teaspoon dried basil
- 1 teaspoon dried oregano
- Salt and pepper to taste

Directions:

Preparing the Cannelloni Filling:

1. In a mixing bowl, combine chopped spinach, ricotta cheese, shredded mozzarella, grated Parmesan, beaten egg, minced garlic, dried oregano, salt, and pepper. Mix until well combined.
2. Using a spoon or a piping bag, fill the cannelloni tubes with the spinach and cheese mixture.

Preparing the Tomato Sauce: 3. In a saucepan, heat olive oil over medium heat. Add tomato passata or crushed tomatoes, dried basil, dried oregano, salt, and pepper.

4. Simmer the sauce for about 15-20 minutes, allowing the flavors to meld.

Baking the Cannelloni: 5. Preheat the oven to 375°F (190°C).

6. Spread a thin layer of tomato sauce on the bottom of a baking dish.
7. Arrange the filled cannelloni tubes in the baking dish.
8. Pour the remaining tomato sauce over the cannelloni, ensuring they are well covered.
9. Bake in the preheated oven for 25-30 minutes or until the cannelloni is cooked through and the top is golden.
10. Remove from the oven and let it rest for a few minutes.
11. Serve the Špinačni Kaneloni hot, optionally garnished with additional Parmesan and fresh basil.

Borovničevi Žličniki (Blueberry Dumplings)

Servings: 4

Time: 45 minutes

Ingredients:

For the Dumplings:

- 2 cups fresh blueberries
- 2 cups all-purpose flour
- 1/2 cup milk
- 2 tablespoons unsalted butter, melted
- 1/4 cup granulated sugar
- 1 teaspoon baking powder
- 1/2 teaspoon vanilla extract
- Pinch of salt

For the Topping:

- 4 tablespoons unsalted butter
- 1/4 cup breadcrumbs
- 2 tablespoons powdered sugar (optional)
- Sour cream or whipped cream for serving

Directions:

Preparing the Dumplings:

1. In a large bowl, combine flour, sugar, baking powder, and a pinch of salt.
2. Add melted butter, milk, and vanilla extract to the dry ingredients. Mix until a soft dough forms.
3. Gently fold in the fresh blueberries.

Forming the Žličniki: 4. Using two tablespoons, shape the dough into small dumplings, resembling spoonfuls. Place them on a floured surface.

Cooking the Žličniki: 5. Bring a large pot of salted water to a gentle boil.

6. Carefully drop the dumplings into the boiling water.
7. Cook until the Žličniki rise to the surface, indicating they are cooked. This usually takes about 5-7 minutes.

Preparing the Topping: 8. In a separate pan, melt butter over medium heat.

9. Add breadcrumbs to the melted butter and toast until golden brown.

Serving: 10. Using a slotted spoon, transfer the cooked Žličniki to a serving dish.

11. Drizzle the toasted breadcrumb and butter mixture over the dumplings.

12. Optionally, dust with powdered sugar for a touch of sweetness.

13. Serve warm with a dollop of sour cream or whipped cream.

Šparglji z Mandljevo Omako (Asparagus with Almond Sauce)

Servings: 4

Time: 20 minutes

Ingredients:

For the Asparagus:

- 1 bunch fresh asparagus, woody ends trimmed
- 1 tablespoon olive oil
- Salt and pepper to taste

For the Almond Sauce:

- 1/2 cup almonds, blanched and peeled
- 2 tablespoons olive oil
- 1 clove garlic, minced
- 1 tablespoon lemon juice
- 1/4 cup water
- Salt and pepper to taste

Directions:

Preparing the Asparagus:

1. Preheat the oven to 200°C (400°F).

2. Place trimmed asparagus on a baking sheet. Drizzle with olive oil, and season with salt and pepper. Toss to coat.

3. Roast in the preheated oven for 10-12 minutes or until the asparagus is tender but still crisp.

Making the Almond Sauce: 4. In a blender or food processor, combine blanched almonds, olive oil, minced garlic, lemon juice, water, salt, and pepper.

5. Blend until the mixture reaches a smooth and creamy consistency. Add more water if needed to achieve the desired thickness.

Serving: 6. Arrange the roasted asparagus on a serving platter.

7. Drizzle the almond sauce over the asparagus or serve it on the side as a dipping sauce.

8. Garnish with additional almonds or a sprinkle of fresh herbs if desired.

Zapečena Polenta s Paradižnikom (Baked Polenta with Tomato)

Servings: 4

Time: 1 hour

Ingredients:

For the Polenta:

- 1 cup polenta (cornmeal)
- 4 cups water
- 1 teaspoon salt
- 2 tablespoons unsalted butter
- 1/2 cup grated Parmesan cheese

For the Tomato Sauce:

- 2 tablespoons olive oil
- 1 onion, finely chopped
- 2 cloves garlic, minced
- 1 can (400g) crushed tomatoes
- 1 teaspoon dried oregano
- Salt and pepper to taste
- Fresh basil leaves for garnish

Directions:

Preparing the Polenta:

1. In a large pot, bring 4 cups of water to a boil. Add salt.
2. Gradually whisk in the polenta, stirring continuously to avoid lumps.
3. Reduce heat to low and simmer, stirring frequently, until the polenta thickens and is cooked through (follow package instructions).
4. Stir in butter and grated Parmesan cheese until well combined.
5. Pour the cooked polenta onto a greased baking dish, spreading it evenly. Allow it to cool and set.

Making the Tomato Sauce: 6. In a saucepan, heat olive oil over medium heat. Add chopped onions and sauté until translucent.

7. Add minced garlic to the pan and cook for an additional minute.
8. Pour in crushed tomatoes and dried oregano. Season with salt and pepper. Simmer for 10-15 minutes until the sauce thickens.

Assembling and Baking: 9. Preheat the oven to 180°C (356°F).

10. Spread the prepared tomato sauce over the cooled and set polenta.

11. Bake in the preheated oven for 25-30 minutes or until the edges are golden and the tomato sauce is bubbling.

Garnishing and Serving: 12. Remove from the oven and let it cool for a few minutes.

13. Garnish with fresh basil leaves before serving.

Rižota z Jurčki (Risotto with Porcini Mushrooms)

Servings: 4

Time: 30 minutes

Ingredients:

- 1 cup Arborio rice
- 1/2 cup dried porcini mushrooms, soaked in warm water
- 1 small onion, finely chopped
- 2 cloves garlic, minced
- 1/2 cup dry white wine
- 4 cups vegetable or chicken broth, kept warm
- 2 tablespoons olive oil
- 2 tablespoons unsalted butter
- 1/2 cup Parmesan cheese, grated
- Salt and pepper to taste
- Fresh parsley for garnish

Directions:

1. In a bowl, soak the dried porcini mushrooms in warm water for about 20 minutes. Once rehydrated, drain and chop them.

2. In a large pan or skillet, heat olive oil over medium heat. Add chopped onions and sauté until translucent.

3. Add minced garlic to the pan and cook for an additional minute.

4. Stir in Arborio rice, ensuring each grain is coated with oil and lightly toasted.

5. Pour in the dry white wine and cook until it evaporates, stirring continuously.

6. Begin adding the warm broth one ladle at a time, allowing the rice to absorb the liquid before adding more. Stir frequently.

7. After adding half of the broth, mix in the chopped porcini mushrooms.

8. Continue adding broth and stirring until the rice is creamy and cooked al dente. This process typically takes about 18-20 minutes.

9. Stir in unsalted butter and grated Parmesan cheese. Season with salt and pepper to taste.

10. Remove from heat and let the risotto rest for a couple of minutes.

11. Serve the Rižota z Jurčki hot, garnished with fresh parsley.

Ocvrti Sir s Krompirjem (Fried Cheese with Potatoes)

Servings: 4

Time: 30 minutes

Ingredients:

For the Fried Cheese:

- **4 slices of your favorite cheese (Gouda, Emmental, or similar)**
- **1 cup breadcrumbs**
- **2 eggs, beaten**
- **1/2 cup all-purpose flour**
- **Salt and pepper to taste**
- **Vegetable oil for frying**

For the Potatoes:

- **4 large potatoes, peeled and cut into wedges**
- **2 tablespoons olive oil**
- **1 teaspoon dried rosemary**
- **Salt and pepper to taste**

Directions:

Preparing the Potatoes:

1. Preheat the oven to 220°C (425°F).
2. In a bowl, toss the potato wedges with olive oil, dried rosemary, salt, and pepper until evenly coated.
3. Spread the seasoned potato wedges on a baking sheet in a single layer.
4. Roast in the preheated oven for 25-30 minutes or until the potatoes are golden brown and crispy.

Frying the Cheese: **5. While the potatoes are roasting, prepare the fried cheese.**

6. In three separate bowls, place flour, beaten eggs, and breadcrumbs.
7. Dip each cheese slice into the flour, then the beaten eggs, and finally coat it in breadcrumbs. Ensure an even coating.
8. Heat vegetable oil in a pan over medium heat.
9. Fry the breaded cheese slices for about 2-3 minutes on each side or until golden brown and crispy.
10. Place the fried cheese on a paper towel to absorb excess oil.

Serving: **11. Arrange the fried cheese alongside the roasted potato wedges on a serving platter.**

12. Serve hot, optionally with a side of your favorite dipping sauce.

Bučna Juha (Pumpkin Soup)

Servings: 4

Time: 45 minutes

Ingredients:

- 1 medium-sized pumpkin (about 2-3 pounds), peeled, seeded, and diced
- 1 large onion, chopped
- 2 carrots, peeled and chopped
- 2 cloves garlic, minced
- 1 potato, peeled and diced
- 4 cups vegetable or chicken broth
- 1 cup coconut milk or heavy cream
- 2 tablespoons olive oil
- 1 teaspoon ground cumin
- 1/2 teaspoon ground nutmeg
- Salt and pepper to taste
- Fresh parsley for garnish (optional)

Directions:

1. In a large pot, heat olive oil over medium heat. Add chopped onions and sauté until translucent.

2. Add minced garlic to the pot and cook for an additional minute.

3. Add diced pumpkin, carrots, and potato to the pot. Stir to combine with the onions and garlic.

4. Pour in the vegetable or chicken broth, ensuring the vegetables are fully covered. Bring to a boil.

5. Reduce heat to low, cover the pot, and simmer for about 20-25 minutes or until the vegetables are tender.

6. Use an immersion blender to puree the soup until smooth. Alternatively, transfer the soup in batches to a blender.

7. Return the blended soup to the pot. Stir in coconut milk or heavy cream.

8. Season the soup with ground cumin, ground nutmeg, salt, and pepper. Adjust the seasoning to taste.

9. Simmer for an additional 5-10 minutes to allow the flavors to meld.

10. Ladle the Bučna Juha into serving bowls.

11. Garnish with fresh parsley if desired.

DESSERTS

Potica (Nut Roll)

Servings: 12

Time: 3 hours (including rising time)

Ingredients:

For the Dough:

- 4 cups all-purpose flour
- 1/2 cup unsalted butter, melted
- 1 cup warm milk
- 1/2 cup granulated sugar
- 1 packet (2 1/4 teaspoons) active dry yeast
- 3 large eggs

- 1/2 teaspoon salt

For the Nut Filling:

- 3 cups ground walnuts or pecans
- 1 cup granulated sugar
- 1 cup milk
- 1/2 cup unsalted butter, melted
- 1 teaspoon vanilla extract
- 1 teaspoon ground cinnamon

Directions:

Preparing the Dough:

1. In a small bowl, combine warm milk and sugar. Sprinkle the yeast over the mixture, stir, and let it sit for about 5-10 minutes until frothy.
2. In a large mixing bowl, combine the melted butter, eggs, and salt. Add the yeast mixture and mix well.
3. Gradually add the flour, mixing continuously until a soft dough forms.
4. Turn the dough onto a floured surface and knead for about 10 minutes until it becomes smooth and elastic.

5. Place the dough in a greased bowl, cover with a kitchen towel, and let it rise in a warm place for about 1-1.5 hours or until it doubles in size.

Preparing the Nut Filling: **6. In a saucepan, combine ground nuts, sugar, milk, melted butter, vanilla extract, and ground cinnamon.**

7. Cook over medium heat, stirring constantly, until the mixture thickens. Remove from heat and let it cool.

Assembling and Baking: **8. Preheat the oven to 180°C (356°F).**

9. Roll out the risen dough on a floured surface into a large rectangle.
10. Spread the cooled nut filling evenly over the dough.
11. Carefully roll the dough into a log, sealing the edges.
12. Place the rolled dough into a greased baking pan, shaping it into a circle or oval.
13. Bake in the preheated oven for 30-40 minutes or until the Potica is golden brown.
14. Remove from the oven and let it cool before slicing.

Optional: **15. Dust with powdered sugar before serving for a decorative touch.**

Kremšnita (Custard Slice)

Servings: 8

Time: 2 hours (including chilling time)

Ingredients:

For the Dough:

- **2 sheets of puff pastry (store-bought or homemade)**

For the Custard Filling:

- **4 cups whole milk**
- **1 cup granulated sugar**
- **1 cup all-purpose flour**
- **6 large egg yolks**
- **2 teaspoons vanilla extract**
- **Zest of 1 lemon**

For the Topping:

- **Confectioners' sugar for dusting**
- **Optional: Whipped cream**

Directions:

Preparing the Puff Pastry:

1. Preheat the oven according to the instructions on the puff pastry package.
2. Roll out the puff pastry sheets on a floured surface, if needed, to fit a baking sheet.
3. Place the rolled-out puff pastry on a baking sheet lined with parchment paper.
4. Bake the puff pastry sheets according to the package instructions or until golden brown and puffed. Allow them to cool completely.

Making the Custard Filling: **5. In a saucepan, heat the milk until it's warm but not boiling.**

6. In a separate bowl, whisk together sugar, flour, and egg yolks until well combined.
7. Gradually add the warm milk to the egg mixture, whisking continuously to prevent lumps.
8. Pour the mixture back into the saucepan and cook over medium heat, stirring constantly, until it thickens.
9. Remove from heat and stir in vanilla extract and lemon zest.
10. Allow the custard to cool to room temperature.

Assembling the Kremšnita: **11. Place one baked puff pastry sheet on a serving platter.**

12. Spread the cooled custard evenly over the first layer of puff pastry.

13. Carefully place the second puff pastry sheet on top of the custard, creating a sandwich.

14. Chill the Kremšnita in the refrigerator for at least 1-2 hours to set.

Finishing Touches: **15. Before serving, dust the top of the Kremšnita with confectioners' sugar.**

16. Optionally, top with whipped cream.

17. Slice into squares or rectangles and serve chilled.

Prekmurska Gibanica (Prekmurje Layer Cake)

Servings: 12

Time: 3 hours (including baking and cooling time)

Ingredients:

For the Dough:

- **2 cups all-purpose flour**
- **1/2 cup unsalted butter, softened**
- **1/4 cup sugar**
- **1/2 cup sour cream**
- **1 large egg**
- **1 teaspoon baking powder**
- **Pinch of salt**

For the Filling Layers:

- **1 1/2 cups cottage cheese (skuta)**
- **1 1/2 cups poppy seeds, ground**
- **1 1/2 cups walnuts, finely chopped**
- **1 1/2 cups apples, peeled and grated**
- **1 cup sugar**
- **1 teaspoon vanilla extract**

- 1 teaspoon ground cinnamon
- 1/2 cup raisins (optional)
- 1/2 cup butter, melted

Directions:

Preparing the Dough:

1. In a large mixing bowl, combine flour, softened butter, sugar, sour cream, egg, baking powder, and a pinch of salt.
2. Knead the dough until it becomes smooth and elastic. Divide it into four equal parts.

Preparing the Filling Layers: **3. In separate bowls, mix cottage cheese, ground poppy seeds, chopped walnuts, grated apples, sugar, vanilla extract, ground cinnamon, and raisins (if using).**

Assembling Prekmurska Gibanica: **4. Preheat the oven to 180°C (356°F). Grease a baking dish.**

5. Roll out one portion of the dough into the size of the baking dish and place it at the bottom.
6. Spread a layer of cottage cheese filling over the dough.

7. Repeat the process, alternating between dough and different fillings, until you use up all the ingredients. Finish with a layer of dough on top.

8. Pour the melted butter over the top layer of dough.

Baking: 9. Bake in the preheated oven for 45-55 minutes or until the top is golden brown.

10. Allow the Prekmurska Gibanica to cool before slicing.

11. Optionally, dust with powdered sugar before serving.

Medenjaki (Honey Gingerbread)

Servings: Approximately 24 cookies

Time: 2 hours (including chilling and baking time)

Ingredients:

- 2 1/2 cups all-purpose flour
- 1/2 cup unsalted butter, softened
- 1/2 cup honey
- 1/2 cup brown sugar
- 1 large egg
- 1 teaspoon ground ginger
- 1 teaspoon ground cinnamon
- 1/2 teaspoon ground cloves
- 1/2 teaspoon baking soda
- 1/4 teaspoon salt
- Zest of 1 orange (optional, for extra flavor)

For the Glaze:

- 1 cup powdered sugar
- 2 tablespoons milk
- 1/2 teaspoon vanilla extract (optional)

Directions:

Preparing the Dough:

1. In a large mixing bowl, cream together softened butter, honey, and brown sugar until light and fluffy.
2. Add the egg and continue to beat until well combined.
3. In a separate bowl, whisk together flour, ground ginger, ground cinnamon, ground cloves, baking soda, and salt.
4. Gradually add the dry ingredients to the wet ingredients, mixing until a dough forms.
5. If desired, add the orange zest to the dough and mix until evenly distributed.
6. Divide the dough into two portions, shape each into a disc, wrap in plastic wrap, and chill in the refrigerator for at least 1 hour.

Baking the Medenjaki: **7. Preheat the oven to 180°C (356°F) and line baking sheets with parchment paper.**

8. On a floured surface, roll out one portion of the chilled dough to a thickness of about 1/4 inch.
9. Use cookie cutters to cut out desired shapes and transfer them to the prepared baking sheets.
10. Repeat the process with the second portion of the dough.
11. Bake in the preheated oven for 8-10 minutes or until the edges are lightly golden.

12. Allow the Medenjaki to cool on the baking sheets for a few minutes before transferring them to a wire rack to cool completely.

Making the Glaze: **13. In a bowl, whisk together powdered sugar, milk, and vanilla extract (if using) until smooth.**

14. Drizzle the glaze over the cooled cookies.
15. Allow the glaze to set before serving.

Jabolčni Zavitek (Apple Strudel)

Servings: 8

Time: 1.5 hours (including baking time)

Ingredients:

For the Dough:

- 2 cups all-purpose flour
- 1/2 cup warm water
- 2 tablespoons vegetable oil
- 1 teaspoon white vinegar
- Pinch of salt

For the Filling:

- 4 large apples (such as Granny Smith), peeled, cored, and thinly sliced
- 1/2 cup granulated sugar
- 1 cup breadcrumbs
- 1 cup ground walnuts
- 1 teaspoon ground cinnamon
- Zest of 1 lemon
- 1/2 cup raisins (optional)
- 1/2 cup unsalted butter, melted

For Dusting:

- Powdered sugar

Directions:

Preparing the Dough:

1. In a large mixing bowl, combine flour and a pinch of salt.
2. In a separate bowl, mix warm water, vegetable oil, and white vinegar.
3. Gradually add the wet ingredients to the flour, stirring continuously until a dough forms.
4. Knead the dough on a floured surface until it becomes smooth and elastic. Cover with a cloth and let it rest for 30 minutes.

Preparing the Filling: **5. In a bowl, combine sliced apples, granulated sugar, breadcrumbs, ground walnuts, ground cinnamon, lemon zest, and raisins (if using).**

6. Preheat the oven to 180°C (356°F).

Assembling the Strudel: **7. Roll out the rested dough on a floured surface into a thin rectangle.**

8. Brush the rolled-out dough with melted butter.

9. Spread the apple filling evenly over the entire surface of the dough.

10. Carefully roll the dough, enclosing the apple filling, and place it on a parchment-lined baking sheet with the seam side down.

11. Brush the top of the strudel with more melted butter.

Baking: 12. Bake in the preheated oven for 35-40 minutes or until the strudel is golden brown and the apples are tender.

13. Remove from the oven and let it cool for a few minutes.

For Dusting: 14. Dust the Apple Strudel with powdered sugar before serving.

Trdinka (Hardened Cream)

Servings: 6-8

Time: 2 hours (including chilling time)

Ingredients:

- 2 cups heavy cream
- 1 cup granulated sugar
- 1 teaspoon vanilla extract
- Fresh berries for garnish (optional)

Directions:

1. In a saucepan, heat heavy cream over medium heat until it just begins to simmer. Do not let it boil.
2. Add sugar to the simmering cream, stirring continuously until the sugar dissolves completely.
3. Reduce the heat to low and let the mixture simmer gently for about 1.5-2 hours, stirring occasionally. The cream will thicken and gradually turn a light golden color.
4. Remove the saucepan from heat and stir in vanilla extract.
5. Allow the mixture to cool slightly before pouring it into individual serving dishes or a larger mold.
6. Refrigerate for at least 4 hours or overnight until the cream hardens.

7. Optional: Serve with fresh berries on top for a burst of fruity flavor.

Šmorn (Kaiserschmarrn)

Servings: 4

Time: 30 minutes

Ingredients:

- 2 cups all-purpose flour
- 1 1/2 cups milk
- 4 large eggs, separated
- 1/4 cup granulated sugar
- 1 teaspoon vanilla extract
- Pinch of salt
- 4 tablespoons unsalted butter
- Powdered sugar for dusting
- Optional toppings: Fruit preserves, apple sauce, or fresh berries

Directions:

1. In a mixing bowl, whisk together flour, milk, egg yolks, sugar, vanilla extract, and a pinch of salt until you get a smooth batter.
2. In a separate clean and dry bowl, beat the egg whites until stiff peaks form.

3. Gently fold the beaten egg whites into the batter until well combined. The batter should be airy.

4. In a large skillet or pan, melt 2 tablespoons of butter over medium heat.

5. Pour half of the batter into the skillet, spreading it evenly.

6. Allow the batter to cook until the edges set and the bottom is golden brown. Then, using a spatula, flip the Šmorn into smaller pieces.

7. Add the remaining 2 tablespoons of butter and pour the remaining batter over the flipped Šmorn. Cook until the second side is golden brown.

8. Using the spatula, continue to break the Šmorn into smaller, bite-sized pieces as it cooks.

9. Once both sides are golden and the inside is cooked through, transfer the Šmorn to a serving plate.

10. Dust the Šmorn with powdered sugar.

11. Serve hot with your choice of toppings, such as fruit preserves, apple sauce, or fresh berries.

Riževa Puding (Rice Pudding)

Servings: 4

Time: 1 hour

Ingredients:

- 1/2 cup Arborio rice
- 4 cups whole milk
- 1/2 cup granulated sugar
- 1 teaspoon vanilla extract
- 1/4 teaspoon ground cinnamon (optional)
- Pinch of salt
- Raisins (optional)
- Zest of 1 lemon (optional)
- Ground nutmeg for garnish (optional)

Directions:

1. In a medium-sized saucepan, combine rice, milk, sugar, vanilla extract, ground cinnamon (if using), and a pinch of salt.
2. Optional: If you'd like, add raisins and lemon zest for extra flavor.

3. Bring the mixture to a gentle boil over medium heat, stirring frequently to prevent the rice from sticking to the bottom of the pan.

4. Once the mixture reaches a boil, reduce the heat to low and let it simmer. Continue stirring occasionally.

5. Simmer for about 30-40 minutes or until the rice is cooked, and the mixture thickens to a creamy consistency.

6. Remove the saucepan from heat and let the rice pudding cool slightly.

7. If desired, sprinkle ground nutmeg on top for garnish.

Krofi (Slovenian Doughnuts)

Servings: Approximately 12 doughnuts

Time: 2 hours (including rising and frying time)

Ingredients:

- 4 cups all-purpose flour
- 1 cup whole milk, lukewarm
- 1/2 cup granulated sugar
- 1/3 cup unsalted butter, melted
- 3 large eggs
- 1 teaspoon vanilla extract
- Zest of 1 lemon
- 1/2 teaspoon salt
- 2 1/4 teaspoons (1 packet) active dry yeast
- Vegetable oil for frying
- Powdered sugar for dusting

Directions:

Preparing the Dough:

1. In a small bowl, combine lukewarm milk and sugar. Stir until the sugar is dissolved, then add the active dry yeast.

Let it sit for about 5-10 minutes until the mixture becomes frothy.

2. In a large mixing bowl, combine flour and salt. Make a well in the center.

3. Pour the yeast mixture into the well, followed by melted butter, eggs, vanilla extract, and lemon zest.

4. Mix the ingredients to form a dough.

5. Knead the dough on a floured surface for about 10 minutes until it becomes smooth and elastic.

6. Place the dough in a greased bowl, cover it with a clean kitchen towel, and let it rise in a warm place for about 1 hour or until it doubles in size.

Shaping and Frying Krofi: 7. **Punch down the risen dough and roll it out on a floured surface to about 1/2-inch thickness.**

8. Using a round cutter or a glass, cut out circles from the dough.

9. Place the dough circles on a baking sheet lined with parchment paper, cover them with a kitchen towel, and let them rise for another 30 minutes.

10. In a deep pan or fryer, heat vegetable oil to 350°F (175°C).

11. Carefully fry the risen doughnuts a few at a time, turning them until both sides are golden brown. This usually takes about 2-3 minutes per side.

12. Use a slotted spoon to remove the fried doughnuts and place them on a paper towel to absorb excess oil.

Finishing Touches: **13. Dust the Krofi with powdered sugar while they are still warm.**

14. Let them cool slightly before serving.

Grmada (Layered Pancake Dessert)

Servings: 8-10

Time: 1.5 hours (including pancake preparation and assembly)

Ingredients:

For the Pancakes:

- **2 cups all-purpose flour**
- **2 cups milk**
- **2 large eggs**
- **2 tablespoons melted butter**
- **Pinch of salt**
- **Butter or oil for cooking**

For the Filling:

- **2 cups ground walnuts**
- **1 cup granulated sugar**
- **1 cup heavy cream**
- **1 teaspoon vanilla extract**
- **1/2 cup raisins (optional)**

For the Topping:

- Whipped cream
- Chocolate shavings or cocoa powder

Directions:

Preparing the Pancakes:

1. In a bowl, whisk together flour, milk, eggs, melted butter, and a pinch of salt until you have a smooth pancake batter.
2. Heat a skillet or pancake pan over medium heat and lightly grease with butter or oil.
3. Pour a small amount of batter into the pan, swirling it to create a thin, even layer. Cook until the edges start to lift, then flip and cook the other side. Repeat until you have a stack of thin pancakes.
4. Allow the pancakes to cool.

Preparing the Filling: 5. In a mixing bowl, combine ground walnuts, granulated sugar, heavy cream, vanilla extract, and raisins (if using). Mix well to create a thick, creamy filling.

Assembling Grmada: 6. On a serving plate, place one pancake as the base.

7. Spread a layer of the walnut filling over the pancake.

8. Continue layering pancakes and walnut filling until you use all the pancakes, finishing with a layer of the walnut filling on top.

9. Optionally, spread some whipped cream on the top layer.

Finishing Touches: **10. Garnish the Grmada with chocolate shavings or dust with cocoa powder.**

11. Chill the layered pancake dessert in the refrigerator for at least 1 hour to allow the flavors to meld.

12. Slice and serve chilled.

MEASURES

1. Volume Conversions:
   - 1 cup = 240 milliliters
   - 1 tablespoon = 15 milliliters
   - 1 teaspoon = 5 milliliters
   - 1 fluid ounce = 30 milliliters
2. Weight Conversions:
   - 1 ounce = 28 grams
   - 1 pound = 453 grams
   - 1 kilogram = 2.2 pounds
3. Temperature Conversions:
   - Celsius to Fahrenheit: $F = (C \times 9/5) + 32$
   - Fahrenheit to Celsius: $C = (F - 32) \times 5/9$
4. Length Conversions:
   - 1 inch = 2.54 centimeters

- **1 foot = 30.48 centimeters**
- **1 meter = 39.37 inches**

5. **Common Ingredient Conversions:**

- **1 stick of butter = 1/2 cup = 113 grams**
- **1 cup of flour = 120 grams**
- **1 cup of sugar = 200 grams**

6. **Oven Temperature Conversions:**

- **Gas Mark 1 = 275°F = 140°C**
- **Gas Mark 2 = 300°F = 150°C**
- **Gas Mark 4 = 350°F = 180°C**
- **Gas Mark 6 = 400°F = 200°C**
- **Gas Mark 8 = 450°F = 230°C.**

Made in United States
·Troutdale, OR
11/21/2024

25123540R00071